Author: Darchelle Tholmer.

Illustrated by: Carla Dirinot.

I got the monday Bluez

Darchelle Tholmer.

Abra the Hungry Alligator opened one sleepy eye.
The sun was up, the birds flew by. He could hear his mommy calling from the kitchen.
But Abra just pulled up the sheets and gave a BIG sigh.
"No school today. I'm staying in bed!"

Mommy peeked in with a smile so wide,
"Time to get up, the sun is shining!"
Abra groaned and buried his head deep in his covers
"I've got the Monday Bluez," he said.

"No socks, no shoes," he grumbled low.
 "No brushing teeth, I don't wanna move my feet!"
 Mommy just chuckled and handed his shoes—
 "We can't let school miss out on you!
 Your friends are ready to run and play."

Abra wiggled and rolled in bed.
"Why do I have to get up?" he said.
"I don't want to get out of bed.
Can't I just stay under my comfy sheets?"

"Time to brush and shine your teeth," Mommy said.
"Let's wake that sleepy alligator head!"
"But I just wanna lay, lay, lay...
Don't wanna play, play, play. I have the Monday Bluez, Abra said.

Abra stared at the ceiling above.
I'm just not feeling today.
My spikes are limp, my tail in a knot,
Getting ready felt like... a lot!

The alarm had rung, and Mommy sang,
"A new week's here—let's give it a bang!"
But Abra hit snooze not once but twice,
"I need more sleep... or maybe some fish!"

"Oh Abra," laughed Mommy, "don't you see?
School is where you should be!"
School is where your friends will be with bright shining faces!
You'll see! You'll jump, jump, jump, and clap, clap, clap,
Stomp your feet, wiggle and sap!"
The fun will carry you through the day.

Abra blinked and scratched his chin.
"Could dancing help my mood begin?"
He tapped one foot, then gave a spin—
The Monday Bluez started wearing thin!

He swayed and snapped, and with each groove,
Abra found his Monday moves.
He smiled and twirled with cheer so bright—
The Monday Bluez were out of sight!

Abra zipped up and shouted, "Yay!"
"I'm ready to learn, play, and conquer the day!"
He hugged Mommy with a happy tune,
"I'll be back home later, but not too soon!"

With a pep in his step. With a groove in his feet.
Abra was ready to take a seat.
His teeth so bright, and his tail held high,
Abra waved and said goodbye.
He skipped to class, with his mood brand new.
There was no signs of those Monday Bluez!

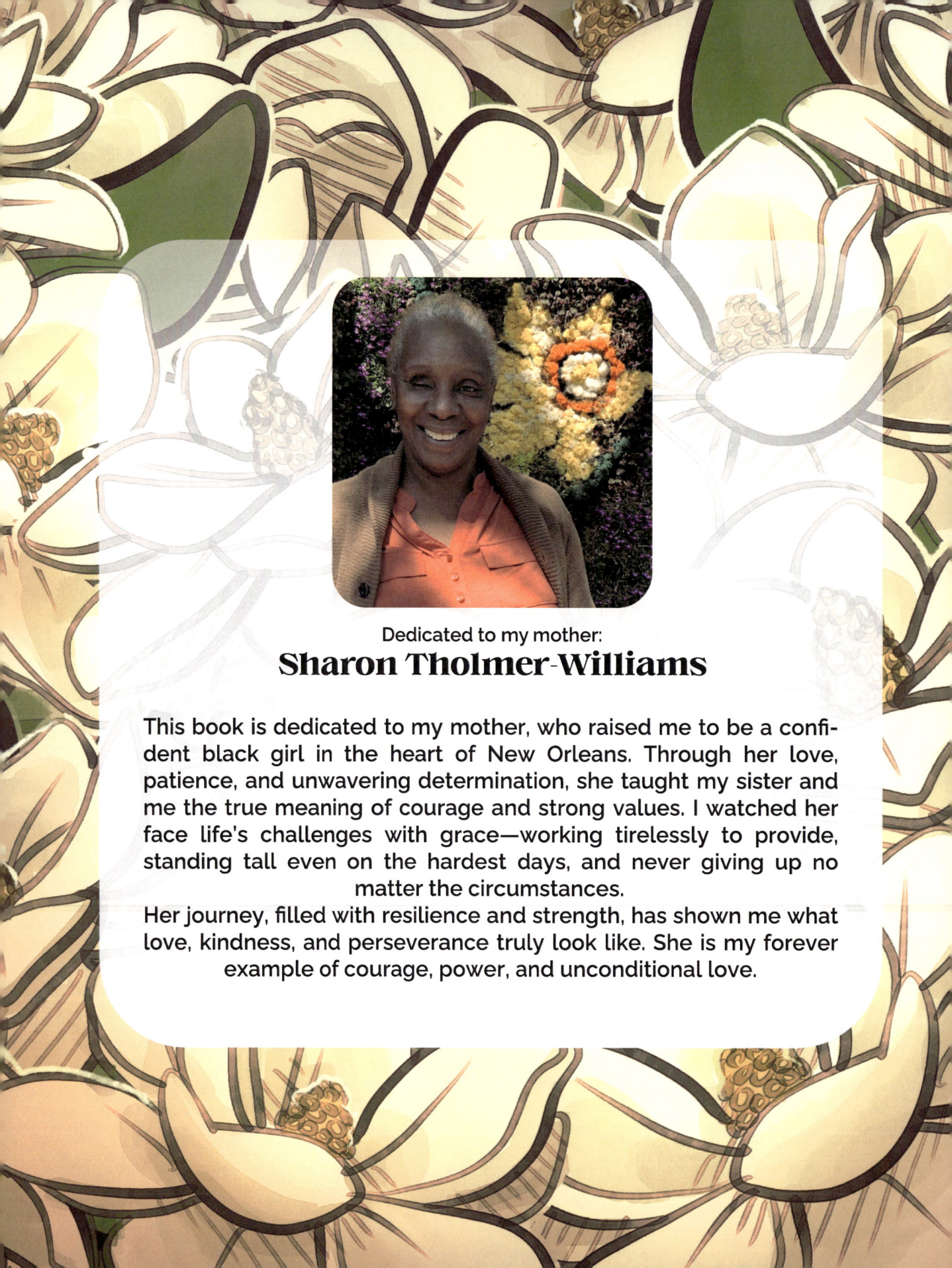

Dedicated to my mother:
Sharon Tholmer-Williams

This book is dedicated to my mother, who raised me to be a confident black girl in the heart of New Orleans. Through her love, patience, and unwavering determination, she taught my sister and me the true meaning of courage and strong values. I watched her face life's challenges with grace—working tirelessly to provide, standing tall even on the hardest days, and never giving up no matter the circumstances.

Her journey, filled with resilience and strength, has shown me what love, kindness, and perseverance truly look like. She is my forever example of courage, power, and unconditional love.

The author:
Darchelle Tholmer.

Darchelle Tholmer is a passionate educator, children's author, and songwriter with over 28 years of experience in early childhood education. She is the creative mind behind **Hungry Alligator** and **Monday Bluez**, stories that help children navigate big emotions through fun, music, and affirmations. As a Fast Track Trainer through Louisiana Pathways, Darchelle also provides professional development for educators, focusing on social-emotional learning and conscious discipline. When she's not writing or teaching, she enjoys spending time with her two dogs, Luka and Chase, and creating meaningful learning experiences for children everywhere.

www.ingramcontent.com/pod-product-compliance
Lightning Source LLC
Chambersburg PA
CBRC091203070526
44583CB00008B/186